A Hymn in My Heart

Dr. James E. Martin

ISBN:

978-1-79486-816-8

Copyright © 2020

by Dr. James E. Martin

No portion of this book may be copied or reproduced in any manner without express, written permission from the author.

INTRODUCTION

Many of us grew up in an era where going to church was a normal way of life. It was not an option. Parents, in many cases, did not simply drop us off at church but took us there and was involved in seeing to it that we did not misbehave but were paying attention to the singing and preaching. Sadly, this is not a reality in many places today.

While there on a typical Sunday morning, one of the many things that I remember so vividly from my own childhood was the singing. How incredibly amazing it was. The hymns were so vibrant and Scripturally complete. They prepared the heart, (yes even many immature hearts), for the preaching that was to follow.

In today's user-friendly church scenes in so many places, the above described scenario is pretty much non-existent. True, this is not always typical, but the modern-day experience seems to be much different. Many of the newer, "more relevant" songs in church services leave much to be desired to many of us old-timers. Please do not misunderstand me here. I am not saying that, just because it is new it is, automatically poor. It is just that so many of the newer songs are extremely weak scripturally. I am sure that many readers will disagree with my analysis.

In this collection I have gathered many "favorites" from people from all walks of life. These will be listed in alphabetic order based on the contributors last name.

In addition to the listing, I will also be providing a brief history of some of the hymns and the circumstances regarding the writing of the song, as well as lyrics to the ones I can confirm are in public domain. This will be found in a separate section, after the listing of favorites. I will probably not list this information (possibly brief history, if found) to the more well-known hymns -- but possibly will as space will allow.

I would like, now, to thank each person who has contributed to this effort. The response, especially the first day or two, has been amazing. I also would like to thank Creed Stone, a friend and co-worker who suggested that I undertake this project.

I pray that, as you read the following pages, you will see much that stirs up many memories in your own heart that will cause you to rejoice for the privilege you had over the years to avail yourself of these great hymns that, perhaps, was used of the Lord to bring you to Christ. May He be praised.

Jim

CONTRIBUTORS

Attison, Roy

Bean, Nancy Kepler

Bean, Ronald

Beard, Debbie Davis

Bell, Jon

Bump, William & Connie Guy

Cassatt, Craig

Choat, Beverly

Cummings, Malcolm

Dimon, Bill

Dechant, Phyllis Goode

Dierking, Debbie

Duncan, Terry

Dunn, Santha Drummond

Gaulkner, Gordon F

Fore, Roger

Frushour, Pat Jones

Gardner, Jan Pretlove

Gillespie, Janice Putman

Gottshall, Brian

Gross, Chuck

Hager, Mike and Jeanne

Hassert, Ted

Hedrick, Sarah & Bob

Hewitt, Jane

Hilterbrand, Diana Smith

Hood Gena

Horner, Glenna

Jaeger, Sharon Chestnut

Johnson, Cathy

Johnson, Greta

Johnson, Ken Bear

Johnson, Vicky Gainer

Kepler, Donna

King, Gina Peterson

LaBelle, Michelle Sylvia

Loggins, Steve

Lyon, Pam Abbott

Martin, Dr. James E.

McCullar, Joy Uptain

McGee, Tim & Deanne

Mooney, Barbara Pretlove

Moore, Dianne Perry

Morgan, Carrie Harbaugh

Neaves, Loretta

Ng, Joseph

Paputsa, Jennifer

Pickering, Sherri Barko

Radin, Ben

Rathbun, Lisa Perry

Reinhold, Rita

Roberts, Marty Payne

Rogers, Don

A Hymn in My Heart

Root, Carolyn

Scott, James W.

Sewell, Gloria

Smith, Esther

Smith, Tanya Hannah

Sorrell, Janelle Hernden

Stallings, Lanette Jones

Stokes, Beth Fowler

Stone, Creed

Summerall, Denise Melanson

Sutherland, Linda

Tan, Mary

Thompson, Valerie Lyles

Watson, Linda

Wear, Jerilyn Duke

Wheeler, Miriam

Attison, Roy

It Is Well With My Soul

by H. G. Spafford

When peace, like a river, attendeth my way,
When sorrows, like a sea billows roll;
Whatever my lot, Thou hast taught me to say,
It is well, it is well with my soul.

Tho' Satan should buffet, tho' trials should come,
Let this blest assurance control,
That Christ hath regarded my helpless estate,
And hath shed His own blood for my soul.

My sin— oh, the bliss of this glorious thought—
My sin— not in part but in whole,
Is nailed to His cross and I bear it no more,
Praise the Lord, praise the Lord, oh, my soul.

And Lord, haste the day when the faith shall be sight,
The clouds be rolled back as a scroll,
The trumph shall resound, and the Lord shall descend,
"Even so"— it is well with my soul.

Chorus

It is well with my soul,
It is well, it is well with my soul.

Sweet, Sweet Spirit

Come Thou Fount

There is a Fountain

Bean, Nancy Kepler

"My Faith Looks Up to Thee" had never been a long-time favorite but became very dear to me in the weeks leading up to and through my Dad's final illness. The last night of his life I was alone with him in the hospital and after talking to him I sang the last verse:

When ends life's transient dream,
When death's cold, sullen stream
Shall o'er me roll,
Blest Savior, then, in love,
Fear and distrust remove;
O bear me safe above, A ransomed soul!

Ten minutes later he went to heaven. We played it for him at his funeral. It has been a tremendous comfort through the

years of remembrance since that time!
Also - Strong in Salvation

Bean, Ronald

Dr. Bob Jr. hymn story: He was never a big fan of the Sword of the Lord, John R. Rice, etc. but maintained a working and somewhat cordial relationship with them. When they published "Soul Stirring Songs and Hymns" (which has very few hymns in it) the asked well-known preachers for their favorite hymns to be included. Dr. Bob Jr. chose "Come Ye Disconsolate, Where'er Ye Languish" saying "I'm pretty sure no one who uses this hymnbook will ever sing this."

Beard, Debbie Davis

The Old Rugged Cross
In the Garden

Bell, Jon

"Complete In Thee"—every single verse is saturated with the gospel!

Even Amazing grace with a full choir and a bagpipe band can't move me like hearing the University Hymn sung in the FMA. It overpowers me every single time!

"Wisdom of God we would by thee be taught. Control our minds, direct our every thought. Knowledge alone, life's problems cannot meet. We learn to live while sitting at thy feet!"

1. On a hill far away stood an old rugged cross,
    The emblem of suff'ring and shame;
   And I love that old cross where the dearest and best
   For a world of lost sinners was slain.
   So I'll cherish the old rugged cross,
   Till my trophies at last I lay down;
   I will cling to the old rugged cross,
   And exchange it some day for a crown.

2. O that old rugged cross, so despised by the world,
    Has a wondrous attraction for me; For the dear
   Lamb of God left His glory above
   To bear it to dark Calvary.
    So I'll cherish the old rugged cross,

Till my trophies at last I lay down; I will cling to the old rugged cross,

And exchange it some day for a crown.

3. In that old rugged cross, stained with blood so divine,
A wondrous beauty I see,
For 'twas on that old cross Jesus suffered and died,
To pardon and sanctify me.
So I'll cherish the old rugged cross,
Till my trophies at last I lay down; I will cling to the old rugged cross,
And exchange it some day for a crown.

To the old rugged cross I will ever be true;
Its shame and reproach gladly bear;
Then He'll call me some day to my home far away,
Where His glory forever I'll share.

So I'll cherish the old rugged cross,

 Till my trophies at last I lay down;

I will cling to the old rugged cross,

And exchange it some day for a crown.

Words: George Bennard, 1913. Music and Setting: 'The Old Rugged Cross' George Bennard, 1913. copyright: public domain. This score is a part of the Open Hymnal Project, 2010 Revision.

Bump, William & Connie Guy

Both "I'd Rather have Jesus" and "Nearer, Still Nearer" really express my heart's cry and have blessed and challenged me many times.

Cassatt, Craig

I have so many favorite hymns; however, the one which I would say is my favorite is "The Prodigal Son". This song reminds me no matter how often or how far away from His service or Grace we may wander, He is always there waiting with open arms to welcome us home again and how God does not stop seeking to bring us back into fellowship with Him.

Choat, Beverly

I have claimed Daddy's favorite song, which was "Amazing Grace" and now for a good many years, is also mine.

Cummings, Malcolm

The Bob Jones University Hymn is just great!

Dimon, Bill

Precious Lord Take My Hand

Dechant, Phyllis Goode

It was my privilege to play for a special service in the early seventies at Greenwood Village Baptist Church in Houston, Texas. Bill Harvey led the music, and Dr. John R. Rice preached his well-known sermon, "The Grapes of Eshcol" from Deut. 1 and Joshua 14:12. Bill Harvey sat on the front pew and I thought he was taking notes. During the invitation when the congregation was standing, he made his way to the piano and put his 'notes' in front of me. He quietly hummed the tune while Dr. Rice was still closing

the invitation. Then Bro. Harvey announced the sermon had inspired him to write a new song and he sang "I Want That Mountain". After a couple of verses, he asked the congregation to join him on the chorus. They loved it. The words remain a delight to me to this day since it challenges us to go on to bigger and better things for God: I WANT THAT MOUNTAIN.
—Phyllis Goode Dechant, BJU Class of 1960.

Dierking, Debbie

I have always liked My Song by Dr. Bob Jr. The chorus says:
So my song must swell the chorus
While the angels' praises ring.
I, a sinner saved and pardoned,
Have more cause than they to sing.

Dunn, Santha Drummond

Just As I Am," the invitational song sung at a revival service when I strongly felt the tugging of God's Holy Spirit urging me to go forward and surrender my life to Jesus, and I did, at the age of 10.

Just As I Am O Lamb Of God

by Horace L. Hastings

Just as I am, O Lamb of God,
Now I come, now I come;
To wash me in Thy cleansing blood,
Now I come, Now I come.
While mercy's guiding beacons beam
To point me to the crimson stream
That makes the foulest sinners clean,
Now I come, Now I come.

Just as I am, without delay,
Now I come, now I come;
To Christ the true and living Way,
Now I come, now I come.
For pardon purchased on the tree,
For grace and mercy rich and free,
O lamb of God, I come to Thee,
Now I come, now I come.

"Kumbaya" . Special song in late 60's/70's. Our youth group enjoyed singing it as we would sit around a campfire. Some of our youth felt, & accepted the call to serve during those special, Holy Spirit felt, times.

"Ready." It had words that were always special to me as I took the words seriously, and I still do.

Duncan, Terry

When we were on campus during one of the 90s' Gold Rush Daze I was moved to tears when everyone sang "Nearer, Still Nearer" acapella. I knew the song from having sung it many times growing up. But this time...I heard the words, words that deeply touched me. To this day, I cannot hear the hymn without crying. The second verse has become my prayer...

"Nearer, still nearer, nothing I bring,
naught as an offering to Jesus my King -
only my sinful, now contrite heart;
grant me the cleansing thy blood doth impart,
grant me the cleansing thy blood doth impart."

Faulkner, Gordon F

AMAZING GRACE Makes me weep when consider the price that was paid for my soul!

Amazing Grace

by John Newton

Amazing Grace, how sweet the sound,
That saved a wretch like me.
I once was lost but now am found,
Was blind, but now I see.

T'was Grace that taught my heart to fear.
And Grace, my fears relieved.
How precious did that Grace appear
The hour I first believed.

Through many dangers, toils and snares
I have already come;
'Tis Grace that brought me safe thus far
and Grace will lead me home.

The Lord has promised good to me.
His word my hope secures.
He will my shield and portion be,
As long as life endures.

Yea, when this flesh and heart shall fail,
And mortal life shall cease,
I shall possess within the veil,
A life of joy and peace.

When we've been here ten thousand years
Bright shining as the sun.
We've no less days to sing God's praise
Than when we've first begun.

Fore, Roger

* I have several favorite hymns and songs, some of the songs were actually hymns and other were of the gospel nature, I do not always know the difference from a technical point of view, but some of the ones listed below are a few of my favorite songs:

* I lean heavily towards the old traditional songs that I grew up with that have [to me, in my opinion] more spiritual and feeling in them than the new contemporary songs. There may be a few contemporary songs that I have heard that I like, but I do not recall the names of the songs at present. The collection of hymns that were advertised on TV several years ago called "101 Greatest Hymns" are one of my favorite collections and also "The Smokey Mountain Jubilee Choir".

Listed below [to me] are just 15 of the many greatest of hymns and songs ever written:

[A.] Just as I Am – [This is or was one of the standard invitational songs that was always played at that time. It has a special meaning to me because it was the song played when I was saved and gave my life to Christ at 13].

[B.] Amazing Grace

[C.] What a Friend We Have in Jesus

[D.] I'LL Fly Away

[E.] Whispering Hope

[F.] How Great Thou Art

[G.] Blessed Assurance

Blessed Assurance

by Fanny J. Crosby

Blessed assurance, Jesus is mine!
Oh, what a foretaste of glory divine!
Heir of salvation, purchase of God,
Born of His Spirit, washed in His blood.

Perfect submission, perfect delight,
Visions of rapture now burst on my sight;
Angels descending, bring from a bove
Echoes of mercy, whispers of love.

Perfect submission, all is at rest,
I in my Saviour am happy and blest;
Watching and waiting, looking above,
Filled with His goodness, lost in His love.

Refrain

This is my story, this is my song,
Praising my Saviour all the day long;
This is my story, this is my song,
Praising my Saviour all the day long

[H.] Rock of Ages

Rock Of Ages

by Augustus Toplady

Rock of ages, cleft for me,
Let me hide myself in thee;
Let the water and the blood,
From the wounded side that flowed,
Be of sin the double cure—
Save me, Lord and make me pure.

Should my tears forever flow,
Should my zeal no langour know,
This for sin could not atone;
Thou must save, and thou alone:
In my hand no price I bring;
Simply to thy cross I cling.

While I draw this fleeting breath,
When my eyelids close in death,
When I rise to worlds unknown.
And behold thee on thy throne—
Rock of Ages, cleft for me,
Let me hide myself in thee!

[I.] All Hail the Power of Jesus Name

[J.] The Old Rugged Cross

[K.] Great Is Thy Faithfulness

[L.] He The Pearly Gates Will Open

[M.] Sweet Hour of Prayer

[N.] Where The Soul Never Dies

[O.] Precious Memories

* When I hear these types of songs, especially when sang with a large choir and organ, I feel like I am soaring through the heavens with the angels getting ready to meet The Lord.

* There are so many of the old songs that I like I cannot remember them all, but some of my favorites are listed above that bring back a lot of good memories back when the churches both large and small were full of people that had decent morals and cared about what God thought, trying to live right, having joy and giving Praise and Glory to God. I think the number one problem with our country is spiritual, our country needs to return back to God.

* Your new book idea sounds very good and I hope it turn out well and a big seller. Maybe it will bring some recognition from religious communities, organizations, individuals and many churches as well. Who knows, there may be some people that will get their life right with God before it is too late, if they heard some of these good songs along with some fire and brimstone preaching.

Frushour, Pat Jones

Two of my favorites are Blessed Assurance & It is Well with my Soul. The 1st one was sung at my Dad's memorial services because it brings back memories of my childhood & him waving his Bible in the air when we got to the chorus "THIS is my story" . . . The 2nd was sung at my Mom's memorial service. I bawled through it during the service because of the truth that I realized when we sang "It is well with my soul"! My Mom passed away July 19,2016 and my Dad passed away November 3,2016.

Gardner, Jan Pretlove

"O, Thou in Whose Presence My Soul Takes Delight" was one of my mother's favorites. We sang it at her funeral.

Gillespie, Janice Putman

Rock of Ages; I've Got That Joy, Joy, Joy, Joy, Down in my Heart

Rock Of Ages

by Augustus Toplady

Rock of ages, cleft for me,
Let me hide myself in thee;
Let the water and the blood,
From the wounded side that flowed,
Be of sin the double cure—
Save me, Lord and make me pure.

Should my tears forever flow,
Should my zeal no langour know,
This for sin could not atone;
Thou must save, and thou alone:
In my hand no price I bring;
Simply to thy cross I cling.

While I draw this fleeting breath,
When my eyelids close in death,
When I rise to worlds unknown.
And behold thee on thy throne—

Rock of Ages, cleft for me,
Let me hide myself in thee!

Gottschall, Brian

"How Great Thou Art" -- Can't sing "Then I shall bow in humble adoration and there proclaim, "My God, how great Thou art" without looking forward to that day when we kneel before Christ Himself.

Also "What a Day That Will Be!"
I printed and framed the words to "Am I a Soldier of the Cross?" I was challenged by the phrase "Must I be carried to the skies
On flowery beds of ease, While others fought to win the prize,
And sailed through bloody seas?"

At a time when I considered leaving the ministry for better financial gains, that hymn challenged me to continue as I realized that I couldn't quit doing what God has called me to do when I considered the greater sacrifices of the martyrs over the centuries. A more comfortable financial position in this life would be great loss if it took me out of God's will.

Hager, Mike & Jeanne

This is a beautiful hymn in which the text and music match perfectly. Definitely a favorite. I thank God for the memories of Dr. Bob and Dr. Gus!   (written in reference to Strong In Salvation

Gross, Chuck

Hello Dr. Martin. I am responding to your solicitation of favorites for your anticipated hymnbook project. I have several in mind and will continue to zap emails to you as they come to mind! Therefore:
1. The Savior is Waiting, Carmichael
2. He Will Hold Me Fast (original tune)
3. Master the Tempest is Raging
4. Dwelling in Beulah Land (far away the noise of strife, etc.)
5. What a Day That Will Be (when my Jesus I shall see, etc.)
6. Sweet Jesus Sweet Jesus (what a wonder you are, etc.)
7. His Wonderful Look of Love, Peterson
8. If We Could See Beyond Today

9. Lovest Thou Me? Gaither

10. In the Same Wonderful Way

11. There's Going to be a Meeting in the Air

12. Overshadowed (by His mighty love, etc.)

13. If I could Sing a Thousand Melodies

14. The Song of the Soul Set Free

15. Yesterday, Today, Tomorrow (Don Wyrtzen)

16. Wonderful, Wonderful Jesus (in the heart he implanteth a song etc.)

17. Something for Thee (Savior Thy dying love etc.)

18. Nothing Between (my soul and the Savior etc.)

19. Yes, He Did (He took my feet from the miry clay etc.)

20. The Great Judgment Morning (had come and the trumpet had blown etc.)

21. Through it All (I've learned to trust Jesus etc.)

22. Come Ye Disconsolate

23. I Hear Thy Welcome Voice (I am coming Lord, coming now to Thee, Wash me, cleanse me, etc.)

24. Jesus Rock of Ages (let me trust in Thee, Jesus Rose of Sharon, etc.)

25. An Old Account Was Settled (long ago and the record, etc.)

26. Gentle Shepherd (come and lead us for we need you

to help us, etc.)

27. I Love You Lord (and lift my voice to worship, etc.)

28. Far Away in the Depths of my Spirit (peace, peace, wonderful peace etc.)

29. Remind Me Dear Lord (roll back the curtains etc.)

30. Wonderful Birth to a Manger He Came (wonderful name He bears etc.)

31. Wonderful Grace of Jesus (just to make sure if no one else said it)

32. Great is Thy Faithfulness

33. It's in His Name (as in Majesty Hymns #115)

34. Where Could I Go (living below in this old sinful world etc.)

35. Well, if I get just one choice for the book, I shall choose Master the Tempest is Raging. What a reflection this is on the Lord of all creation! (Note: This was in response to my question to Chuck regarding what his choice would be if he were to only pick one song. Great choice!!)

Hager, Mike &Jeanne

Probably the University Hymn. Dr. Bob perfectly expressed his aspirations for the university named for his father.

Hassert, Ted

Praise Ye Jehovah and the University Hymn!

Hedrick, Sarah & Bob

After God got me through a very difficult time in my life, I was singing "How Firm a Foundation" with our church's congregation. I had never noticed the fifth verse (and it isn't in many hymnals). "The soul that on Jesus hath leaned for repose, I will not, I will not, desert to its foes. That soul, though all Hell should endeavor to shake, I'll never, no, never, no, never forsake!" Aaah! So good!

Hewitt, Jane

"I'll fly away" It is the promise of the future. Sung at many funerals. I think as a final testimony of the person who has passed.

Hilterbrand, Diana Smith
(written in response to Lisa Rathbun's submission)
I was saved at 4 years old, and I went through the same doubts at   times. I love this hymn, too! Someday we will know our "spiritual birthdays" "when we all get to

heaven!"

Hood, Gena

"Jesus Paid it All" - - because it says it all.

Horner, Glenna

I love so many hymns (many that I learned as a student at BJU that I had never heard in my own church), but "When I Survey the Wondrous Cross" is definitely a favorite. When I consider all that Jesus has done for me through His suffering and death, "Love so amazing, so divine, demands my soul, my life, my all!"

In the early years of our marriage, in a small church in southwestern Pennsylvania, an elderly lady who was quickly becoming a dear friend of ours, asked my husband to sing "Safe in the Arms of Jesus" as a special for her sister who was even older than she and closer to Heaven. We had never heard of that hymn by Fanny Crosby, but my husband, Tim, learned it and sang it for these sweet ladies. Since then, it has been a hymn that comes to mind in times of trial and the passing of friends and loved ones who are believers.

Johnson, Cathy

Rejoice in the Lord by Ron Hamilton. I remember when Ron sang it at Bible Conference during one of the afternoon sessions. It was so moving you could hear a pin drop in the amphitorium. That was March 1979. It made a huge impression on me as a sophomore in college.

Jaeger, Sharon Chestnut

When my husb. was being rushed to the hosp. with a heart attack, I felt so numb. I didn't know how to feel, or to process my thoughts. The hymn "Come Thou Fount" meant so much with the words" Prone to wander, Lord I feel it-,, prone to leave the GOD I love, Here's my heart, oh take and seal it, seal it for Thy courts above,,," That fountain, of words meant so much!---still ministers to me today!!!

Tune my heart!!!!

Johnson, Greta

Like a river glorious.... is God's perfect peace. Words that I think on, sing, remember when I'm in life's stresses.

***Dianne Perry Moore** YES! This is my society song!

Johnson, Ken Bear

How about "How Can I Keep From Singing"
I am a hymn history buff and have quite a collection of hymn history books. I would really like to have this one to learn about some new hymns and add to my collection.

Johnson, Vicky Gainer

It is well with my soul

Kepler, Donna

A song that I have known all my life - and hadn't heard or sung for years, now that so many churches have given up so many of the older songs - is "Now I Belong to Jesus". About a year ago I heard somebody playing it on the piano as a postlude, and the words came back to my mind. For the first time, the truth of the words "Jesus belongs to me" really sank in. It was one thing to know that I belong to Jesus, and I love knowing that, but the realization that the "ownership" (so to speak) is mutual was a revelation!

King, Gina Peterson

What a Lovely Name

LaBelle, Michelle Sylvia

I have many favorites; my mom was the oldest of 7 children and at night they sang hymns together instead of watching tv, so my mom made sure I learned many hymns as well. My mom died of cancer age 58. When she was on her deathbed her brother Charlie and his wife Marlene, who had a music ministry, came to the house one day and my aunt and uncle, mom, and myself sang hymn after hymn from memory with my uncle playing guitar. After about an hour of singing, my uncle asked my mom if she had any last requests, and she said "The Sweet By and By." My uncle said he wasn't sure he could remember all the words to that one but we would try. We made it through the first verse and faded out on the second except for my mom who kept singing the second verse and halfway through her singing the third verse my uncle knelt down by her bed tears coming down his face and said Big sister, why'd you request this song? You knew this was going to happen. And he hugged her and kissed her and told her how much he was going to miss her; said his goodbyes right there. Touched my heart so much. A couple years later my daughter worked on a beautiful piano arrangement of The Sweet By and By- I cried a lot when she was practicing it, and she played it for her high school piano recital.

Also, I also really like the Doxology. I've had people tell me they don't like it because it's just sung in tradition and nobody thinks about the words. But for me it's different. I grew up as a pastor's daughter. I sat in the very first pew every Sunday morning; we would have the offering and we would stand and sing the Doxology as the men would bring the offering plates back to the communion table where I could practically count the offering from where I sat. And as a kid I was thankful because part of that offering was how my dad got paid. But the church people loved God and gave- many of the people in that church my dad personally led to Jesus as Savior. My piano teacher made me memorize a beautiful rendition of the Doxology because she said every church pianist should be very familiar with it. The church I attend now rarely sings it, and I miss it.

When I was a little girl we sang hymns as well as choruses in Sunday School. One of those hymns was "He Lives." I love this song and think it is unfortunate that it is usually only sung around Easter. In a way this song is very appropriate for the world we live in today where most young people live by feelings instead of truth, so they may not want to listen to the truth of God's Word, but it is hard for them to deny when there's been a true change for the better in your life, and that change is brought about because Jesus lives.

When I was a kid we used to go to a nursing home service once a month, and we would sing all the really old hymns like Rock of Ages, The Old Rugged Cross, And Can It Be, Blessed Assurance, What a Friend We Have in Jesus. My dad said the old people, especially those with dementia and Alzheimer's, liked the old songs because they had grown up singing them and they were familiar with them.

Loggins, Steve
One of my favorite hymns is "He Hideth my Soul" written in 1890 by Fanny J. Crosby. It is based on Exodus 33:22.

Lyon, Pam Abbott
Wall of Prayer. It is special to me because my church came to my house when my dad was dying and sang to him. The

words are wonderful.

How Great Thou Art

Martin, Dr. James E.

The list of favorites is long and growing every day. I am "old school", meaning that I love the older, traditional hymns that have been around for year, many for hundreds of years. One of my favorites is, "My faith Has Found a Resting Place". The lyrics to this one, in addition to multitudes of others, is a wonderful theology describing the amazing possession of the believer. The words, "I need no other argument, I need no other plea; It is enough that Jesus died, And that He died for me.", sum up concisely the attitude that a believer should portray each and every day.

McCullar, Joy Uptain

What a friend we have in Jesus. He is my reason for all I do.

McGee, Tim N Deanne

Oh, what a Savior and When I bowed on my knees and cried holy- my Dad's favorites and sung and played at his funeral

Mooney, Barbara Pretlove

"Write"!!

Praise Ye Jehovah is one I love. It's in Hymns of Grace and Glory.

Moore, Dianne Perry

"Beulah Land" has become a song that I hold dear to my heart! It speaks of our longing for a better place and the promise that we will be in that place when we die. That sing has become a must at family funerals. We had it played at all 4 of our parents' funerals.

My "pastor" of over 45 yrs, Rev. Norman Pyle, entered heaven's gates a yr or 2 ago (my memory fails me on the date). A few weeks after his passing a short video clip was played at our church with what was said to be his last "sermon" to our church. The song was "God will take care of you" and that is a wonderful promise to us who are left behind!

Morgan, Carrie Harbaugh

Farther Along is a favorite. As it reminds me even though I don't understand current circumstances, He sees the picture.

Some things I may not understand till heaven.

"Shall We Gather At The River" was always sang when someone got baptized at my childhood church. It's a rejoicing song over a soul saved.

"Nearer Still Nearer" reminds me of BJU.

> *****Beth Fowler Stokes** Loved singing "Nearer, Still Nearer" at BJU. Beautiful

> *****Pat Jones Frushour** Acapella in FMA is the best!

Neaves, Loretta

A Mighty Fortress Is Our God and I Walk Through the Garden Alone (may not be the title)

Oh God Forgive Us

Ng, Joseph

I don't have one but multiple favorites, and for various reasons, including several that are Canadian, one that's sentimental from growing up years, a couple that were favourites of close friends, but all in protest to the Charismatic culture pervading Christendom. "O worship the Lord in the beauty of holiness;" sentimental from my dad's slum ministry; "Glorious things of thee are spoken" for my late co-pastor John S. Winter and his mom's and deaf-blind nephew's fave "Guide Me O Thou Great Jehovah" and "This is My Father's World" respectively, and my little collection of hymns Canadian https://drive.google.com/open...

Paputsa, Jennifer

The Lord used "Rock of Ages" to help assure me of His saving work in me. "Thou must save and thou alone."

Pickering, Sherri Barko

Definitely, the University Hymn!

Radin, Ben

Dear Dr. Jim,

I am Ben Radin BJU '61. I've been in Chr.School Admin. until retirement and have just turned 79. I am glad to hear that someone is going to do a project with the great hymns! It seems today that most folks are sacrificing them on the "Contemporary" altar of musical pablum. Some time ago I made my own listing of "Favorite Hymns"....about 130 of them. I like lots more, but these were favorites. You asked for "perhaps several" so I list nine:

A Mighty Fortress is My God - Written by Martin Luther and a hymn the early church grew upon exponentially

And Can It Be - Learned to love it while at BJU --- powerful message

BJU University Hymn -Learned to love it while at BJU - again, great music and powerful words

The Cleansing Wave - A favorite for over 50 years...learned it early in my ministry at a time when my spiritual growth was accelerating

Hallelujah, What a Savior - A favorite of my brother, Teed Radin, a Navigator - shared it with me before he passed away in an auto accident

I am Not Skilled to Understand - Another I learned to love from my brother

I Love to Tell the Story - Learned to love it when it was the theme song of Back to the Bible Broadcast which we listened to frequently - great missions message

Lord, Speak to Me - Learned to love it in our church at a time of missions emphasis when my heart was especially sensitive to doing the will of God

The Bible Stands - This one goes back to the early 1960's when our small country church was growing fast and the emphasis on the impact of God's Word was so striking

Keep us posted! God bless you as you embark on this great project! In Christ, Ben Radin

Rathbun, Lisa Perry

I Love "How Firm a Foundation." Having come into contact with preachers who demanded things like you had to remember the date of your salvation or you had to be emotionally moved or you had to see a huge change in your life (a difficult thing when you asked Christ to be your savior when you are very young), I struggle with doubts for years. This song reminds me that my faith is in Christ based on the word of God, not on something I did or said or might have felt. My assurance is based in His Word.

Some of the lyrics are based directly on Bible verses. It's such a wonderful message of faith and hope to hold on to in the darkest times.

Reinhold, Rita

"How Can It Be?" sung outside of the Amphitorium during Bible conference. It stirs my soul.

Roberts, Marty Payne

"The Love of God" : My dad had sung this as a solo a few times, though he was not a soloist. He requested it to be sung by man with a strong voice at his funeral. It was sung by Missionary Dick Knox. Dad also requested "What A Friend", which was played on musical instrument by several family members. So both are special to me.

"University Hymn" - at graduation & "Strong In Salvation" - as sung by Mrs. Gustafson!!!!!

Rogers, Don

So many to choose from.... It is Well with My Soul must win out though.

The verse "My sin, oh the bliss of this glorious thought, my sin not in part but the whole, is nailed to the cross, and I bear it no more, Praise the Lord, Praise the Lord oh my soul." After years of feeling condemned because of my sin nature due to a legalistic church and the mental abuse there, I came to the true realization of the full completeness of grace and Christ's work totally beyond the scope of my sin----OH the Bliss---If only I have had this assurance and knowledge years ago.

Root, Carolyn

During a sermon at Bible Conference Dr. John R. Rice sang "O To Be Like Thee" with tears flowing down his cheeks. That was in the '60s, and his sincerity made a big impression on me.

Scott, James W.

Not really a hymn, but I love to hear Ralph Stanley sing this ol' 1951 song

(written in 1913). The song reminds me there is no peace

anywhere

without complete faith in the Lord.

No church, no friend, no family member can succeed in giving me

peace of spirit and mind. Only He can do that, and that will not work

without me surrendering to His Station and Sovereignty.

A man of sorrow becomes without sorrow when he or she arrives

at constant remembrance of the Lord and His Love for us.

Sewell, Gloria

I suppose my favorite hymn would have to be "Just As I Am" for many reasons. It was of course the Hymn we all were singing when I walked down that aisle, having walked the stairs from our balcony with tears running down my face to publicly profess that I wanted to give Jesus my all. Pastor Billy Graham, whom we just lost to Heaven's Glory, had it sung at all of his meetings around the world. But the words are what grabs and holds. "Just as I am!" I don't need to do anything more than be His child because He loved me first, foremost and always. To be a child of the King has been my comfort for all these many years.

It's time to sing one of the old, old favorites 🎼 "I'd Rather Have Jesus"

The background of the song is as sweet as the song it's self- ☺

Although American hymnals show Rhea Miller as the author of this song, Swedish sources attribute the original to Prince Oscar Bernadotte. In 1888 he relinquished his royal title and right to succession in order to marry a commoner who had influenced his religious beliefs. Afterward he was active in Christian service.

🎼 George Beverly Shea sang it at many of Billy Graham's Crusades 🎼

I'd rather have Jesus than silver or gold;
I'd rather be His than have riches untold;
I'd rather have Jesus than houses or lands;
I'd rather be led by His nail-pierced hand
Refrain:
Than to be the king of a vast domain
Or be held in sin's dread sway;

A Hymn in My Heart

I'd rather have Jesus than anything

This world affords today.

I'd rather have Jesus than men's applause;

I'd rather be faithful to His dear cause;

I'd rather have Jesus than worldwide fame;

I'd rather be true to His holy name

Refrain:

Than to be the king of a vast domain

Or be held in sin's dread sway;

I'd rather have Jesus than anything

This world affords today.

He's fairer than lilies of rarest bloom;

He's sweeter than honey from out the comb;

He's all that my hungering spirit needs;

I'd rather have Jesus and let Him lead

Refrain:

Than to be the king of a vast domain

Or be held in sin's dread sway;

I'd rather have Jesus than anything

This world affords today.

Smith, Esther

Just as I am--I was saved at age 11 at a revival singing that song. Frank was the Music director for the revival. 2 Beyond the Sunset, with the narrative: Should you go first-- sang at my mother's funeral.

Standing on the Promises – another favorite of my mother's

Smith, Tonya Hannah

Jesus I Am Resting Resting became very close to me when my husband had a massive stroke at the age of 39. Definitely a time of learning His greatness and resting in Him

Sorrell, Janelle Hernden

How Firm A Foundation speaks of our assurance that God will keep His promises, then enumerates them

Stallings, Lannette Jones

Because He Lives

Victory in Jesus

In The Garden

When He Was On The Cross

One Day At A Time

Stokes, Beth Fowler

"Be Thou My Vision"

The message of this song is the desire of my heart. Because it is my favorite, I had it sung during our wedding.

Stone, Creed

Come Thou Fount of Every Blessing

Be Thou My Vision

…my grandfather would hum or sing this all the time (old Irish hymn translated)

I love the Lord – be still my soul. A para phrase of 2 Nehi 4:16-35 from the Book of Mormons. Could not find just the lyrics ,but read the words. Would be good song for the Warblers.

The Lord's Prayer played at lights out (bed time) at Camp Sumatanga.

Summerall, Denise Melanson

I love the chorus to "Finally Home"

"But just think of stepping on shore
And finding it Heaven
Of touching a hand
And finding it God's
Of breathing new air
And finding it celestial
Of waking up in glory
And finding it Home!"

Sutherland, Linda

I love "Strong in Salvation"" too
(written in reference to Strong In Salvation)

Tan, Mary

Sorry for the delay in reply, for I was too lazy to send you a long one immediately. But for me, it has to be "What a Friend We Have in Jesus". It was the first hymn I ever learned in my life and I learned the Chinese version all by myself when I was in elementary school. My parents are non-believers but my dad had a friend who visited Hong Kong in the early 1980s and gave my family a Chinese Bible and a Chinese-English pamphlet entitled "Living Water" as gifts. The pamphlet included the full text of the Gospel of John, as well as the hymn. I loved the gifts very much as a child, but my parents told me not to take them to my school, and said something like "They are considered to be imperialistic here and you might get into trouble." I took them to school, anyway, and lost them both eventually. But prior to that, I had learned to sing the hymn all by myself. But I did not become a Christian until I was 20, for the Communist world view was(and yes, unfortunately, it still is) the only thing being taught in China's public schools. Had I had Christian parents who could explain the Gospel to me earlier, or had this country had real religious freedom, I would have become a Christian much earlier. Thanks.

In Christ,
Tan, Xin (Mary Tan)

Note: Mary is a believing Christian who lives in China. She teaches in a University there.

Thompson, Valerie Lyles

I was 26, my husband was in seminary, and I was teaching in a Christian school, serving the Lord ON MY TERMS. I didn't want the Lord to send me to a place where I would be uncomfortable 😊 :) During a seminary graduation service, God broke my heart with the song, "Lord, Send Me Anywhere," David Livingstone's words set to music by Faye Lopez. Life is short, souls are dying, I want my life to count for Christ. Surrendering my will to His made me SO much more comfortable!

Watson, Linda

Dr Jim,

First off, I would like to thank you for your service to our country! My brother served 23 yrs. in the Army. He was in a tank maintenance division and was stateside during Desert Storm.

Now for those favorite hymns.

1. **The Wonder of It All** (by George Bev Shea) It was my dad's favorite song and I think of him every time I hear it. One day I heard it at least 3 times. The phrase that is so overwhelming in scripture is connected to this song:

"...before the foundation of the world... (HE LOVED ME!!!)"

2. **Goodnight** by Ron Hamilton. I played this song a lot during my mom's short illness prior to her 'homegoing'. Ron's dad had Alzheimer's Disease, and this song sort of brings this out. Three verses depict 3 eras' in his life...as a child his dad sang this song, now Ron sings it to Dad, then it ends in heaven. (Ron is now suffering the onset of Alzheimer's).

3 A favorite for me...**Keep the Race Before Us**, again by Ron Hamilton, helps remind me the reason we serve Christ and that God knows what is going on in our lives. This song helped me through several work-related downsizing and eventual closing of our facility, ending my 40-year nursing career.

4. One more: **He Leadeth Me**. it always brings tears so that I can't sing it. Am I really letting HIM lead me? Am I willing?

Hope this helps. I am a 1985 BSN graduate from BJU. I worked at Barge for 26.5 yrs. before it closed in 2014.

A Hymn in My Heart

Linda Watson

Build Faith, Challenge Potential, Follow Christ

I Timothy 4:12-16

Wear, Jerilyn Duke

How Great Thou Art....My Dad would ask me to play it every night growing up....so I requested it to be one of the songs for his Funeral in 2016.

Wheeler, Miriam

"May the Mind of Christ my Savior". Powerful lyrics that challenge me to daily walk with God. Special to me as a missionary doctor because some stanzas deal especially with sharing the Good News and compassionate healing. Often when I have a medical team come to Ukraine from the US, we sing/read this hymn, and there is not a dry eye in the room. "And may they forget the channel, seeing only Him".

Young, Sharon

Dear Dr. Martin -
My what a loaded question you ask :-)

I hope you get many, many responses.

I love many hymns, choruses, and praise songs. But if I had to narrow it down to favorites, I'd probably say my favorites were All That Thrills My Soul Is Jesus and Higher Ground, for the simple reason that they were the first hymns I learned when I was taught to read music. I learned to read words when I was about three. I learned to read music much later. But some things just stick with you. And I still love these two. Doesn't hurt that the lyrics are just plain awesome.

Hope this helps -~~~~~~
Sharon Young
aka satscout

LYRICS

&

HISTORIES

SECTION

In the pages to follow I will be including the lyrics to many of the great old hymns. Many of the newer hymns will not be included because of copyright restrictions. This, in no way, implies that the lyrics to these newer hymns are somehow inferior to the older ones. It is just that the laws governing publication does not allow them to be published. The lyrics to most of the hymns in this book can, however, be found on line by a simple Google search.

Also included in this section will be a few historical facts relating to the timeframe of the writing and some significant statements associated with the writing. Not every hymn will be included because of space restriction, or I was unable to find any recorded historical facts.

Hymn lyrics and histories will be listed in alphabetical order based on title of hymn. Both the lyrics and histories will be poster together. I would highly recommend that you study again the lyrics to these great old hymns. We so often just sing through them and pay little attention to the messages of these songs. So much great theology is often missed as a result.

All That Thrills My Soul is Jesus

Written by Thoro Harris, in 1931.

Thoro Harris, the author of today's hymn, was born in Washington D.C. in 1874. Though nothing is known of his childhood and youth, we pick up his career in Michigan at Battle Creek College, a Seventh-Day Adventist school. He was a gifted songwriter and after graduation moved to Boston to enter the publishing business. In 1902 he produced the first of dozens of hymnals and song collections. In those days Christian publishing was big. As a result of his success, Harris was invited by Peter Bilhorn to move to Chicago. Bilhorn was active in Christian music, working with evangelists Billy Sunday, D.L. Moody, and George Stebbins.

Am I a soldier of the cross

Written by Isaac Watts

The noble hymn that we are to commit to memory was written by Dr. Watts in 1709, to follow a sermon on 1 Corinthians 16:13, "Watch ye, stand fast in the faith, quit you like men, be strong." It is sometimes condensed to four stanzas, but surely, <u>we shall not wish to lose the last two</u>. He died in 1748.

Be Thou My Vision

Mary Elizabeth Byrne translated the Old Irish Hymn, "Bi Thusa 'mo Shuile, into English in 1931

Beulah Land

Written in 1875, 76 by Edgar Page Stites. Made poplular in modern day by Squire Parsons.

Beyond the Sunset

Written by Virgil Brock

>Part of an email conversation posted by Lindsay Terry regarding the writing of this song:

A number of years ago, while serving as Music and Education Director of the Buffalo Avenue Baptist Church in Tampa, Florida, I had an unexpected visit from Brock. I was thrilled, to say the least, and quickly took him into the church's radio studio and recorded his story - the story of how "Beyond the Sunset" was born. I still have the tape of that recording session.

Brock began, "We were watching a sunset over Winona Lake, in Indiana, one evening. With us were two friends, Horace and Grace Burr. Horace had been blind for many years. We went to the dinner table still talking about that impressive sunset. The lake seemed to be ablaze with the glory of God. But above that unusual sunset were threatening storm clouds."

"As we talked about that sunset Horace said, 'I never saw a more beautiful sunset, and I've seen them around the world.' I said, 'Horace, you always talk about seeing.' He said, 'I do. I see through others' eyes, and I think I see more than many others see. I can see beyond the sunset.' I said, 'Horace, that's a great idea for a song, and I began singing: Beyond the sunset, 0 blissful morning, when with our savior heaven is begun."

Blessed Assurance

Written in 1873 by blind writer Fanny Crosby

Come Thou Fount

Written 1757 by Robert Robinson

Perhaps all hymns are to some extent autobiographical in that they reveal something of the author's spiritual experience. In some hymns, the autobiographical thread is stronger and more obvious. Such is the case with British Baptist hymn writer Robert Robinson (1735-1790), who as a barber's apprentice, fell under the powerful influence of George Whitefield's preaching.

A favorite line in the last stanza, "Prone to wander, Lord, I feel it, prone to leave the God I love," is thought to be particularly autobiographical, referring to Robinson's early life, when his mother sent him to London to be an apprentice. It was during this time, according to hymnologist Kenneth Osbeck, that "he associated with a notorious gang of hoodlums and lived a debauched life" until he came under the spell of Whitefield.

After his conversion in 1755, Robinson first preached at a Calvinistic Methodist chapel at Mildenhall, Suffolk, and then founded his own independent congregation at Norwich. He was re-baptized in 1759 after taking up Baptist theological perspectives.

Glorious Things of Thee are Spoken

Written by John Newton (1775-1807)

Newton, John, who was born in London, July 24, 1725, and died there Dec. 21, 1807, occupied an unique position among the founders of the Evangelical School, due as much to the romance of his young life and the striking history of his conversion, as to his force of character. His mother, a pious Dissenter, stored his childish mind with Scripture, but died when he was seven years old. At the age of eleven, after two years' schooling, during which he learned the rudiments of Latin, he went to sea with his father. His life at sea teems with wonderful escapes, vivid dreams, and sailor recklessness. He grew into an abandoned and godless sailor. The religious fits of his boyhood changed into settled infidelity, through the study of Shaftesbury and the instruction of one of his comrades. Disappointing repeatedly the plans of his father, he was flogged as a deserter from the navy, and for fifteen months lived, half-starved and ill-treated, in abject degradation under a slave-dealer in Africa. The one restraining influence of his life was his faithful love for his future wife, Mary Catlett, formed when he was seventeen, and she only in her fourteenth year. A chance reading of Thomas à Kempis sowed the seed of his conversion; which quickened under the awful contemplations of a night spent in steering a water-logged vessel in the face of apparent death (1748). He was then twenty-three. The six following years, during which he commanded a slave ship, matured his Christian belief. Nine years more, spent chiefly at Liverpool, in intercourse with Whitefield, Wesley, and Nonconformists, in the study of Hebrew and Greek, in exercises of devotion and occasional preaching among the Dissenters, elapsed before his ordination to the curacy of Olney, Bucks (1764).

The Olney period was the most fruitful of his life. His zeal in pastoral visiting, preaching and prayer-meetings was unwearied. He formed his lifelong friendship with Cowper, and became the spiritual father of Scott the commentator. At Olney his best works—-*Omicron's Letters* (1774); *Olney Hymns* (1779); *Cardiphonia*, written from Olney, though published 1781—were composed. As rector of St. Mary Woolnoth, London, in the centre of the Evangelical movement (1780-1807) his zeal was as ardent as before. In 1805, when no longer able to read his text, his reply when pressed to discontinue preaching, was, "What, shall the old African blasphemer stop while he can speak!" The story of his sins and his conversion, published by himself, and the subject of lifelong allusion, was the base of his influence; but it would have been little but for the vigour of his mind (shown even in Africa by his reading Euclid drawing its figures on the sand), his warm heart, candour, tolerance, and piety. These qualities gained him the friendship of Hannah More, Cecil, Wilberforce, and others; and his renown as a guide in experimental religion made him the centre of a host of inquirers, with whom he maintained patient, loving, and generally judicious correspondence, of which a monument remains in the often beautiful letters of *Cardiphonia*. As a hymnwriter, Montgomery says that he was distanced by Cowper. But Lord Selborne's contrast of the "manliness" of Newton and the "tenderness" of Cowper is far juster. A comparison of the hymns of both in *The Book of Praise* will show no great inequality between them. Amid much that is bald, tame, and matter-of-fact, his rich acquaintance with Scripture, knowledge of the heart, directness and force, and a certain sailor imagination, tell strongly. The one splendid hymn of praise, "Glorious things of thee are spoken," in the Olney collection, is his. "One there is above all others" has a depth of realizing love, sustained excellence of expression, and ease of development. "How sweet the name of Jesus sounds" is in Scriptural richness superior, and in structure, cadence, and almost tenderness, equal to Cowper's "Oh! for a closer walk with God." The most characteristic hymns are those which depict in the language of intense humiliation his mourning for the abiding sins of his regenerate life, and the sense of the withdrawal of God's face, coincident with the never-failing conviction of acceptance in The Beloved. The feeling may be seen in the speeches, writings, and diaries of his whole life.

(Above copied from www.hymnary.org)

He Leadeth Me

Written by Joseph H. Gilmore

Gilmore, Joseph Henry, M. A., Professor of Logic in Rochester University, New York, was born at Boston, April 29, 1834, and graduated in Arts at Brown University, and in Theology at Newton Theological Institution. In the latter he was Professor of Hebrew in 1861-2. For some time he held a Baptist ministerial charge at Fisherville, New Hampshire, and at Rochester. He was appointed Professor at Rochester in 1868. His hymn, "He leadeth me, O blessed thought" (Ps. xxiii.), is somewhat widely known. It was written at the close of a lecture in the First Baptist Church, Philadelphia, and is dated 1859. It is in the Baptist Hymnal [and Tune] Book, Philadelphia, 1871.

.How Can I Keep From Singing

Also known as:
My Life Flows On in Endless Song

These are the words as published by Robert Lowry in the 1869 song book, *Bright Jewels for the Sunday School*.[3] Here Lowry claims credit for the music, an iambic 87 87 tune[4] with an 87 87 refrain, but gives no indication as to who wrote the words. These words were also published in a British periodical in 1869, *The Christian Pioneer*,[5] but no author is indicated. Lewis Hartsough, citing *Bright Jewels* as source of the lyrics and crediting Lowry for the tune, included "How Can I Keep from Singing?" in the 1872 edition of the *Revivalist*.[6] Ira D. Sankey published his own setting of the words in *Gospel Hymns, No. 3* (1878), writing that the words were anonymous.[7] In 1888, Henry

S. Burrage listed this hymn as one of those for which Lowry had written the music, but not the lyrics.[8]

I Am Not Skilled to Understand

Author: Dora Greenwell (1873)

Greenwell, Dorothy, commonly known as "Dora Greenwell," was born at Greenwell Ford, Durham, in 1821; resided at Ovingham Rectory, Northumberland (1848); Golborne Rectory, Lancashire; Durham (1854), and Clifton, near Bristol, where she died in 1882. Her works include Poems, 1848; The Patience of Hope, 1861; The Life of Lacordaire; A Present Heaven; Two Friends; Songs of Salvation, 1874, &c. Her Life, by W. Dorling, was published in 1885. -- John Julian, Dictionary of Hymnology

In the Garden

C. Austin Miles

"**In the Garden**" (sometimes rendered by its first line "**I Come to the Garden Alone**"[is a gospel song written by American songwriter C. Austin Miles (1868–1946), a former pharmacist who served as editor and manager at Hall-Mack publishers for 37 years. According to Miles' great-granddaughter, the song was written "in a cold, dreary and leaky basement in Pitman, New Jersey that didn't even have a window in it let alone a view of a garden."[1] The song was first published in 1912 and popularized during the Billy Sunday evangelistic campaigns of the early twentieth century by two members of his staff, Homer Rodeheaver and Virginia Asher.

It is Well With my Soul

Words by: Horatio Gates Spafford, 1873.
Music by: Philip Paul Bliss, 1876.

Some of the story may be true, but there's much more to the story before and after the song!

In the 1870s, Spafford was a very successful lawyer in Chicago and heavily invested in real estate. In 1871, the great Chicago fire destroyed all his downtown investment properties.

In 1873, he and his family planned a vacation trip to Europe. While in Great Britain, he planned to help his good friend Dwight L. Moody and Ira Sankey, whom he had financially supported, with their evangelistic tour. Spafford sent his wife and four girls—ages 11, 9, 7 and 2—ahead while he finished up last-minute business in Chicago. On November 22, the S.S. *Ville Du Havre* struck another ship and sank within twelve minutes. Mrs. Spafford cabled her husband "Saved alone."

One story reports that Spafford wrote "It Is Well with My Soul" while passing over the very spot of the ocean where his four daughters perished while another, more reliable report, claims he wrote it two years later when Moody and Sankey were visiting his home.

Jesus I am Resting, Resting

Words: Jean Sophia Pigott (b. Sept. 8, 1845; d. Oct. 12, 1882)

Music: *Tranquility*, by James Mountain (b. July 16, 1844; d. June 27, 1933)

The hymn we'll look at in this post was a favorite of missionary Hudson Taylor, during the Boxer Rebellion in China. Word came to him of one after another of his missionaries being brutally slain. *Jesus, I Am Resting, Resting*, became a great comfort to him and the missionaries around him. They sang it often. Jean Pigott's own brother Thomas, a missionary to China, was killed in the rebellion.

My Faith Has Found a Resting Place

Author: E. E. Hewitt

 Pseudonym: Lidie H. Edmunds. Eliza Edmunds Hewitt was born in Philadelphia 28 June 1851. She was educated in the public schools and after graduation from high school became a teacher. However, she developed a spinal malady which cut short her career and made her a shut-in for many years. During her convalescence, she studied English literature. She felt a need to be useful to her church and began writing poems for the primary department. she went on to teach Sunday school, take an active part in the Philadelphia Elementary Union and become Superintendent of the primary department of Calvin Presbyterian Church

My Faith Looks Up to Thee

Written by Ray Palmer (1830)

O To Be Like Thee

Words: Thomas O. Chisholm, in the *Young People's Hymnal*, 1897.

Music: William J. Kirkpatric

O Worship the Lord in the Beauty of Holiness

Written by John S. B. Monsell (1811- 1875) died from falling from roof of his church

Precious Memories

J. B. F. Wright, author-composer of "Precious Memories" (originally copyrighted in 1925), was born in Tennessee, February 21, 1877. In contrast to the majority of modern-day writers and composers, Mr. Wright has never taught nor does he claim a great amount of music education. He writes from inspiration, and in his own words, "... when words came spontaneously, flowing into place when I feel the divine urge." Mr. Wright is a member of the Church of God, and his writing, as did his church work, began at a very early

Rock of Ages

Text: Augustus M. Toplady, 1740-1778
Music: Thomas Hastings, 1784-1872

There is a legend that Augustus Toplady was inspired to write this hymn after finding shelter from a thunderstorm in a cleft in a rock at Burrington Combe in Somerset, England in 1776. While evidence to support that story is lacking, it does provide a vivid image through which to understand the hymn. Christ and His redemptive work on the cross are like that cleft in the rock, where we can find shelter from the deluge of sin's guilt and power.

Safe in the Arms of Jesus (1868)

Fanny Crosby, music by W. H. Doane

Mr. Doane came into a room in New York, once, where Fanny Crosby was talking with Mr. Bradbury, the father of Sunday-school music, and said to her: "Fanny, I have written a tune and I want you to write words for it."

"Let me hear how the tune goes," she replied. After Mr.

Doane had played it over for her on a small organ, she at once exclaimed: "Why, that tune says, ' Safe in the arms of Jesus,' and I will see what I can do about it."

She at once retired to an adjoining room, where she spent half an hour alone. On returning she quoted to Mr. Doane the words of this now immortal hymn. It was first published in the book entitled "Songs of Devotion."

STRONG IN SALVATION

Dr. Bob Jones Jr. (1911-1997)

Author: Bob Jones, Jr., 1911-1997
Musician: Dwight Gustafson, b. 1930

The Old Rugged Cross

George Bernard (1913)

There is a Fountain

Cowper, William, 1731-1800

Cowper, William, the poet. The leading events in the life of Cowper are: born in his father's rectory, Berkhampstead, Nov. 26, 1731; educated at Westminster; called to the Bar, 1754; madness, 1763; residence at Huntingdon, 1765; removal to Olney, 1768; to Weston, 1786; to East Dereham, 1795; death there, April 25, 1800.

The simple life of Cowper, marked chiefly by its innocent recreations and tender friendships, was in reality a tragedy.

His mother, whom he commemorated in the exquisite "Lines on her picture," a vivid delineation of his childhood, written in his 60th year, died when he was six years old. At his first school he was profoundly wretched, but happier at Westminster; excelling at cricket and football, and numbering Warren Hastings, Colman, and the future model of his versification. Churchill, among his contemporaries or friends. Destined for the Bar, he was articled to a solicitor, along with Thurlow. During this period he fell in love with his cousin, Theodora Cowper, sister to Lady Hesketh, and wrote love poems to her. The marriage was forbidden by her father, but she never forgot him, and in after years secretly aided his necessities. Fits of melancholy, from which he had suffered in school days, began to increase, as he entered on life, much straitened in means after his father's death. But on the whole, it is the playful, humorous side of him that is most prominent in the nine years after his call to the Bar; spent in the society of Colman, Bonnell Thornton, and Lloyd, and in writing satires for *The Connoisseur* and *St. James's Chronicle* and halfpenny ballads. Then came the awful calamity, which destroyed all hopes of distinction, and made him a sedentary invalid, dependent on his friends. He had been nominated to the Clerkship of the Journals of the House of Lords, but the dread of appearing before them to show his fitness for the appointment overthrew his reason. He attempted his life with "laudanum, knife and cord,"—-in the third attempt nearly succeeding. The dark delusion of his life now first showed itself—a belief in his reprobation by God. But for the present, under the wise and Christian treatment of Dr. Cotton (q. v.) at St. Albans, it passed away; and the eight years that followed, of which the two first were spent at Huntingdon (where he formed his lifelong friendship with Mrs. Unwin), and the remainder at Olney in active piety among the poor, and enthusiastic devotions under the guidance of John Newton (q. v.), were full of the realisation of God's favour, and the happiest, most lucid period of his life. But the tension of long religious exercises, the nervous excitement of leading at prayer meetings, and the extreme despondence (far more than the Calvinism) of Newton, could scarcely have been a healthy atmosphere for a shy, sensitive spirit, that needed most of all the joyous sunlight of Christianity. A year after his brother's death, madness returned. Under the conviction that it was the command of God, he attempted suicide; and he then settled down into a belief in stark contradiction to his Calvinistic creed, "that the Lord, after having renewed him in holiness, had doomed him to everlasting perdition" (Southey). In its darkest form his affliction lasted sixteen months, during which he chiefly resided in J. Newton's house, patiently tended by him and by his devoted nurse, Mrs. Unwin. Gradually he became interested in carpentering, gardening, glazing, and the tendance of some tame hares and other playmates. At the close of 1780, Mrs. Unwin suggested to him some serious poetical work; and the occupation proved so congenial, that his first volume was published in 1782. To a gay episode in 1783 (his fascination by the wit of Lady Austen) his greatest poem, *The Task*, and also *John Gilpin* were owing. His other principal work was his *Homer*, published in 1791. The dark cloud had greatly lifted from his life when Lady Hesketh's care accomplished his removal to Weston (1786): but the loss of his dear friend William Unwin lowered it again for some months. The five years' illness of Mrs. Unwin, during which his nurse of old became his tenderly-watched patient, deepened the darkness more and more. And her death (1796) brought "fixed despair," of which his last poem, *The Castaway*, is the terrible memorial. Perhaps no more beautiful sentence has been written of him, than the testimony of one, who saw him after death, that with the "composure and calmness" of the face there "mingled, as it were, a holy surprise."

A Hymn in My Heart

Cowper's poetry marks the dawn of the return from the conventionality of Pope to natural expression, and the study of quiet nature. His ambition was higher than this, to be the Bard of Christianity. His great poems show no trace of his monomania, and are full of healthy piety. His fame as a poet is less than as a letter-writer: the charm of his letters is unsurpassed. Though the most considerable poet, who has written hymns, he has contributed little to the development of their structure, adopting the traditional modes of his time and Newton's severe canons. The spiritual ideas of the hymns are identical with Newton's: their highest note is peace and thankful contemplation, rather than joy: more than half of them are full of trustful or reassuring faith: ten of them are either submissive (44), self-reproachful (17, 42, 43), full of sad yearning (1, 34), questioning (9), or dark spiritual conflict (38-40). The specialty of Cowper's handling is a greater plaintiveness, tenderness, and refinement. A study of these hymns as they stood originally under the classified heads of the *Olney Hymns*, 1779, which in some cases probably indicate the aim of Cowper as well as the ultimate arrangement of the book by Newton, shows that one or two hymns were more the history of his conversion, than transcripts of present feelings; and the study of Newton's hymns in the same volume, full of heavy indictment against the sins of his own regenerate life, brings out the peculiar danger of his friendship to the poet: it tends also to modify considerably the conclusions of Southey as to the signs of incipient madness in Cowper's maddest hymns. Cowper's best hymns are given in *The Book of Praise* by Lord Selborne. Two may be selected from them; the exquisitely tender "Hark! my soul, it is the Lord" (q. v.), and "Oh, for a closer walk with God" (q. v.). Anyone who knows Mrs. Browning's noble lines on Cowper's grave will find even a deeper beauty in the latter, which is a purely English hymn of perfect structure and streamlike cadence, by connecting its sadness and its aspiration not only with the "discord on the music" and the "darkness on the glory," but the rapture of his heavenly waking beneath the "pathetic eyes" of Christ.

To Canaan's Land I'm on my Way

(Known to many as "Where the Soul Never Dies"

Author: William M. Golden

[William Golding] Born: January 28, 1878, Webster County, Mississippi. Died: May 13, 1934, in a traffic accident near Eupora, Mississippi. Buried: Spring Valley Cemetery #2, Mathiston, Mississippi. Son of James and Camella Hood Golding (his surname changed later), it is said he wrote most of his songs while serving an eight-year sentence in the state penitentiary. His only child reportedly died young.

www.ingramcontent.com/pod-product-compliance
Lightning Source LLC
Chambersburg PA
CBHW051712040426
42446CB00008B/840